AF174014

SAVE

OUR

...——...SHIP...——...

SAVE
OUR
...—...SHIP...—...

Poems

Barbara Louise Ungar

 THE ASHLAND POETRY PRESS

Copyright © 2019 by Barbara Louise Ungar

All rights reserved. Except for brief quotations in critical reviews, this book, or parts thereof, must not be reproduced in any form without permission of the publisher. For further information, contact the Ashland Poetry Press, Ashland University, Ashland, OH 44805, www.ashlandpoetrypress.com.

Printed in the United States of America

ISBN: 978-0-912592-74-9

LCCN: 2019944284

Cover art: Joseph Mallord William Turner, used by permission Tate Images, London
Cover design: Nicholas Fedorshak

Author photo: Ben Marvin

Acknowledgments

Love and gratitude to Stuart Bartow, first reader and consort. Also to Margo Mensing, for criticism and encouragement, along with Jon Brown, Alyssa Cohorn, Jackie Craven, Amber Jackson, Susan Kress, Daniel Mandil, Michael Meyerhofer, W. T. Pfefferle, and Leah Umansky. Thank you to Stephen Ellcock for another indelible cover image. Mighty thanks to Deborah Fleming and all at Ashland Poetry Press, and to Mark Jarman, for the honor. Thank you to the College of Saint Rose for support and sabbatical leave, and to my colleague, art historian Theresa Flanigan, for giving me "The Diverse Vices of Women, Alphabetized"—a renaissance alphabet to teach women to control their sensual appetites, especially their desire for speech—which inspired this book.

Grateful thanks to the editors of the following journals where these poems appeared, often in earlier forms:

Anthem: A Tribute to Leonard Cohen: "How the Light Gets In"
Arabesques: "Emily Dickinson's Estate Sale," "How the Light Gets In," "Painlandia,"
     "She Drives Home after Viewing the Drones Quilt"
Atticus Review: "Dear Bill," "Interior Paramour," "MOAB," "Wedding with First
     Boyfriend," "After Zumba"
Blueline: "Lot's Ex"
Borders and Boundaries, Raynes Prize Anthology: "For Vincent Byrne"
Chronogram: "The Woman with a Live Cockroach in Her Skull"
Diaphanous: "Endnotes to Coral Reefs"
Ealain: "Knitting of the Dead"
Facts, Fictions and Fakes, Raynes Prize Anthology: "Shooting into the Hurricane"
Gargoyle: "*Après Moi*," "Man Bun Ken," "Your Mother Serves Tongue"
Green Briar Review: "Quoth the Queane"
La Presa: "Accident Report," "Ode to Ibolya," "Now We Are 15"
The Misfit: "Hand Me Down," "*Jeanne et Moi*," "Souvenir," "The Blues Sister,"
     "Wyndemoan," "X-Wife" (as "Whose Car Is Parked in Your Drive")
Naugatuck River Review: "Positively West Fourth Street"
Painters and Poets: "Venus with a Mirror"
Scoundrel Time: "Cassandra"
Southern Indiana Review: "*Maria Lactans*," "Spiritual Housekeeping"
Thema: "Golden Orb Weaver"

Trailer Park Quarterly: "*Ars Poetica*," "How It Happens"
Two Bridges Review: "On a Scale of One to Ten"
The Worcester Review: "Global Weirding"
Wordpeace: "Rondeau for Shaimaa al-Sabbagh"

For my mother, who read me poetry.

Contents

Language is the only homeland.
—Czeslaw Milosz

Everywhere there is has everything there is to look at.
—Bernadette Mayer

The entirety of this evil, brought upon us by the curse of Eve, is the inspiration...
—St. Antoninus of Florence

The Diverse Vices of Women, Alphabetized

For a woman is an   *Est enim mulier*

Avid animal	*Avidum animal*
Bestial pit	*Bestiale baratum*
Carnal and concupiscent	*Concupiscentic carnis*
Dolorous duel	*Dolorosum duellum*
Ever-burning heat	*Aestuans aestus*
False faith	*Falsa fide*
Garrulous gullet	*Garrulum guttur*
Heinous fury	*Herinnys armata*
Igniting jealousy	*Invidiosus ignis*
Kaleidoscope of calumny	*Kalumnarium chaos*
Luring plague	*Lepida lues*
Mendacious monster	*Monstruosum mendacium*
Nurse of shipwrecks	*Naufragii nutrix*
Odious operator	*Opifex odii*
Primary sinner	*Prima peccatrix*
Quasher of quietude	*Quietis quassatio*
Ruiner of realms	*Ruina regnorum*
Savage in pride	*Silva superbiae*
Truculent tyrant	*Truculenta tyrannis*
Vanity of vanities	*Vanitas vanitatum*
Xerxes' insanity	*Xantia Xersis*
Ymage of idols &	*Ymago idolorum*
Zealous jealousy	*Zelus zelotypus*

Accident Report

.— .— .— .— .—

Love skids slowly into the guardrail
wearing a negligee but no seat belt
tricked by a slick of black ice

The car's wrecked but Love
limps away shivering   crouches in bracken
to call AAA with shaking hands

By the time the tow truck comes
she's borrowed a coat
from a fox who's vamoosed
leaving prints like petals on the snow

Ars Poetica

.— .— .— .—

I love to comb
a poem the way
girls do their dolls'
hair singing

as I brushed
and braided mane
and tail curried
every inch

of the pony
I owned only
in words and rode
naked through town

Après Moi

.— .— .—

Let them eat storms
Let them eat fire
Let them eat drones
Let them eat lies

Let them eat bump stocks
Let them eat coal
Let them eat bullets
Let them eat wall

Let them eat stilettos
Let them eat the lying press
Let them eat tax returns
Let them eat the last jaguar

Let them eat opiates
Let them eat paper towels
Let them eat petrochemical sludge
Let them eat the howling of mothers

Let them eat ashes
Let them eat mold
Let them eat fallout
Let them eat America first

Let them
Eat
Dust

The Other Barbara
—··· —··· —··· —···

Long ago you walked into the desert
slept with Bedouins in their tents
pissed under a full moon on golden sand.
Was that you the women dressed
in their black embroidered robes? Lost snapshot
of her riding camels against a cobalt sky—
where did that other Barbara vanish?

Walking around the frozen lake
you had to stop and sit on a cold stone wall
another Barbara by your side as you slipped
into the parallel world of pain
that underwater world you don't see
till you're in it, astonished
at its teeming reefs.

Fasting, trembling
naked in a worn common gown
tied at the back,
before going under
you meet another Barbara—
euphoric just to be
at home in this smallest house
empty and shining as a shell.

Like a gold ring in the snout, a woman is beautiful and foolish.
— Proverbs 11:22

The Blues Sister
—··· —··· —··· —···

At work that morning, found my handbag
gone. Had to teach and drive home
at night with sunglasses on.
Detoured for accidents
twice, lost on familiar streets
ending up back where I started.
Don't get pulled over
without my license.
Home hours late to a dark
house and the missing bag
on the bed where I left it.

Don't have to replace every thing—
just the lights burned out all over
the house, and no man to help
with the difficult fixture.

Flying dream: a murmuration
of black birds above, can't
flip over to see the lake below—
the flippers are slipping off
my sweaty feet and
how would I get home
without them?
                    Eagles
and carrion birds   drift
among the smaller flocks.

There must be something dead
down there.

Cassandra
—. —. —. —.

watches people stumble down the street talking
loudly to people who aren't there.

Cassandra knows she's
or they're under an enchantment.

Hard to see its exact shape. The hot parts
hotter, vineyards aflame.
Cities underwater.
Archipelagos of plastic trash.
Flotillas of fire ants.

Cassandra pulls at her eyelashes.

Fish forget to eat, mate, flee.
Even the flowers
poisoned. Bats
hang dead in their caves.

Cassandra plucks out her eyebrows
waiting for Clytemnestra to call.

She could light herself on fire.

So many lotus eaters.
What would it take
to wake them up?

The Woman with a Live Cockroach in Her Skull

—. —. —. —. —. —. —. —.

felt a tingling
crawling in her nostril
a burning in her eyes
when it moved Alive
in there full grown
nestled at the base
of the skull

How did it get *in?*

Reading online keeping
her awake at night

How to get it out?

Flummoxed the experts
warn of infection
spreading
            She wakes screaming
each morning at the news

Can this be true
or just some parable

Don't you feel it now too?

Emily Dickinson's Estate Sale

—.. —.. —.. —.. —.. —.. —.. —..

It is not down on any map; true places never are.
—Melville

I got her glasses and sunglasses—
both surprisingly hip—
and a blue fountain pen.

I wanted to head out for the ocean
but you didn't. You were delighted
with her liqueur glasses, delicate
and tall on two glass trays,
and a remote for the ceiling light.

You switched it on—dazzling.
The estate was vast, with lots of visitors
wandering through, yet not crowded withal.
Not the cramped rooms
in Amherst. Her other place.
Not on any map.

Dear Bill

—.. —.. —..

Isn't it great
not being dead yet
you'd say and giggle.

Is it great being dead too?
Lucky, Whitman calls it.

When you were my age
you'd been dead five years.
Unthinkable.
           You are always
ahead, father-brother, with the sad
damage of all the men I love:
It's never not Mom.

Kill the A+ student, don't
get a PhD. Don't keep writing
the same book, start another.
I ignored your advice

yet you remain the teacher
I try to be—so lightly erudite,
wit your scalpel—no one ever
left your class crying.

You never know who in a class
is going to write a great poem
you said and meant it.

Men are worms. Really.
You drank too much
lively with the ladies
dirt beneath your nails
and bags under your eyes.

The only difference between being
moderately well-read and really *well-read*
is insomnia.
　　　　You limped
like me, through marriages,
divorces, single-parenthood.

You called what you did
　　　　　　　Stand-up
tragedy
　　　　the job
schlepping books to readings
as glamorous as that of
a traveling feed salesman.

I'm always late with thank yous,
this one, decades.
　　　　　　In every real poem
　　　　　　someone's heart is breaking.

I missed
your festschrift. You don't care.
You are out of time.

Endnotes to Coral Reefs

. . . .

1. Oases of ocean
2. Nocturnal tube worms, sea stars, sea urchins, feather dusters
3. Underwater cities
4. Hard, stony or reef-building corals secrete a skeletal cup
5. A single coral animal can live a thousand years
6. Coral spawn on only one night a year during a spring full moon
7. Soft corals: black, thorny, horny, sea fan, sea plume, sea pansy
8. All corals are killed by water that is too warm
9. Egg bundles are round—bright red, pink or orange—half the size of small gumballs
10. Stress, pollutants, sediment, acidity, warming oceans, dynamite, poison
11. Budding corals reproduce asexually
12. What sailors called mermaids were likely dugongs
13. Corallite closely resembles human bone
14. Bleaching and subsequent starvation
15. The Great Barrier Reef can be seen from outer space
16. Centuries to build   destroyed in weeks
17. She plunged into the deep blue waters off Kirimati Island
    It is other-worldly
    like it snowed on the reef
    bleached white ghosts popping up off the ocean floor
    We are sticking our heads in the sand

Elegy

. . . .

The 2018 *Oxford Junior Dictionary*
has culled

        acorn

            adder

   ash

      beech

           bluebell

buttercup

         catkin

     conker

                     cowslip

       cygnet

dandelion

          fern

     hazel

               heather

        heron

          ivy

kingfisher

                       lark

          mistletoe

      nectar

newt

                   otter

        pasture

            willow

and added

*attachment block-graph blog broadband bullet-
point celebrity chatroom committee
cut-and-paste MP3 player voice-mail.*

Wedding with First Boyfriend

.. —. .. —. .. —. .. —. .. —. .. —.

After forty years, we know everything
that can and does go wrong—five divorces
between us. The more we drink
and talk, the more his teenaged face

peeks out, a starved cat in the ruins.
The hungry looks I loved slink there—
the eyes, the lips, the joking voice.
He has let himself go.   Go where?

He has settled for a cupboard when we
once owned the very palace
where this young couple shines
arrogantly beautiful and clueless.

When we part, I don't pick up on
his hapless come-on. Yet who ever spent
happier hours than we did then
on that rank couch in the basement?

How was this man defeated, who used to sing
and play me *Lay Lady Lay* on his guitar?
Who, driving to the movies, used to kiss
my fingers in the dark of the car.

Lake George Barns

— —. — —. — —. — —.

The bird clock still ticks
but at random times
the wrong bird sings.

I beat the braided rug
in the snow, sweep
bunny prints from the drive.

Bittersweet's the first plant
ever to speak to me
personally. It said thank you

for the trellis.
Each scarlet aril
in its frilly cap of snow.

A full moon loomed
so huge over an old barn
I almost drove off the road.

When did I first see Georgia O'Keefe's
Lake George Barns? When Dad
first took us to the Walker

I had seen lakes and I had seen barns.
I gazed at those grey-green
and red weathered shapes—

who would name a lake George
and why would a lake have barns?

Global Weirding
— —. — —. — —.

And pluck till time and times are done,
The silver apples of the moon,
The golden apples of the sun.
　　　　　　—Yeats

Some still do not believe
in the weather. Mass

hallucination? Sump pumps,
who'd dream them up?

Crammed in a musty cellar
velvet and cobwebs,

the roundelay of denial.
Our passports to the dreamtime

cancelled. Let the clocks take trains.
Let spacetime bulge around us

like dolphins caught in tuna nets.
Let lobsters let other lobsters out

of lobster pots at the bottom of the sea.
Could those gravitational waves

we heard at last from silver apples
really be the music of the spheres?

Brush Up Your Heidegger

....

Someone's added me to the Martin Heidegger
Facebook Group, where guys post things like
I and me are in deep conversation.

All I can remember from grad school is
What is it to *dwell*? Didn't Heidegger
become a Nazi, or was that Nietzsche?

Nietzsche and Nazi are almost homophones
like *schmuck* and *shtup* or *schlemiel* and *schlemazl*.
(What was Hannah Arendt thinking?) I dig out

"What Are Poets For?" Good question.
To be a poet in a destitute time
means: to attend, singing, to the trace

of the fugitive gods.
                    And Rilke:

    We are the bees of the invisible.

Hand Me Down

....

I knew he would pass me
his pencil marks climbing up
the kitchen doorframe criss-
cross mine slipping down
Still it's strange to wear his out-
grown sneakers or sweatshirt
to look up at him or be picked up
and carried around the house

Under my pillow
an old pj top
night blue jersey
stamped with paler stars
spiral galaxies and spaceships
saved from when he was so new
it seemed impossible he would ever
fill those long sleeves

I keep it to shield my eyes
against that busy old fool
the rising sun
a constant token
of the warp speed of life
and the barely imaginable
stretchings and shrinkings
of spacetime

Helen of Brussels

···· ···· ···· ···· ····

Pat Robertson says there may be demons
lurking in thrift-shop clothes.
In the pocket of my latest

find, a coral rain jacket,
two train tickets:
Ne pas plier S. V. P., and inside

these pliéd tickets, receipts
for *La passion du chocolat*
Rue des Tongres, Bruxelles—

First honeymoon, whirlwind
tour of the great cities of Europe
possessed by delirium of first love

mit schlag, waffles and chocolate
for breakfast in bed... He was more imp
or prick than demon, *en fin*.

The bottom stamped *Servi par Hélène*.
Was this the face that served a thousand jerks?
No wonder this jacket makes me feel so

delicious, like Helen Mirren who said
You can buy a jacket for five hundred bucks
or buy one in a thrift shop, and no one

can tell, so get the thrift-shop jacket
plus a bottle of champagne.

How It Happens
···· ···· ···· ···· ····

Maybe it starts with cheating—he says you drove him to it.
Maybe you yell & hit him thinking you can't hurt him till he
hits back. Maybe his hands around your neck you see crimson
you're choking him back & if there were a gun someone could
be dead. Maybe he throws you across the room somehow
you're out on the street running sniveling everyone steers clear.
Maybe you call someone. Maybe he says it's safe to come
home *it will never happen again*. Maybe he's sorry fills the
house with a hundred roses.

> Maybe it never happens again.
> Maybe it does.

Or maybe he would never cheat. Maybe he doesn't talk for hours
that turn into days. Maybe he won't let you sleep or the baby
nap. Maybe drives drunk won't stop the car when you need to.
Calls you crazy accuses you of cheating parks his car behind
yours so you can't get out. Maybe he wakes you up for sex &
you do it dreaming of sleep. Maybe he throws the bottle at you &
punches a hole in the wall. You need a plan. Maybe you throw
up breakfast for a week. Take the baby & run.

> There are so many ways it can happen.
> It happens all the time.

I Go on the Road of All the Earth

.. ..

—David, dying, to Solomon, I Kings 2.2

Their hair was shorn
in the *HAARESCHNEIDERAUM*

combed out and cured in lofts
over the ovens

gathered into bales
sold to make thread yarn rope

stiffening for uniforms
felted boot liners

socks for submarine crews
pulling them below

Some unruly strands selected
to detonate bombs—

The rest a jumble
of braids and curls remains

heaped in museum vitrines
conserved fumigated

the ultimate proof
turning to dust

   Where did they all go?
   You tell me, where did all these people go?

As you see in Genesis 21, great was Sarah's envy of Hagar...
—St. Antoninus

Interior Paramour

.. ..

Your consort writes
Not a day or night goes by
when I do not think of you

to another woman.
He says he was lying.
You say Then

or now? That night
at last you meet
Him—pale ocean

eyes, red-gold
hair—your hands
touch, smiles near...

He says *This is a good*
problem to have
Being pure light

his radiance
like a jack-o-lantern's
shines from within

even when you wake
weirdly happy
and alone again.

Iguana Sestina
.. ..

I saw them far off in the mist
a tangle of iguanas
flashes of iridescent color.
I was simply looking for food
and then, with luck, housing—
not worrying about the architecture

of this foreign archipelago, if architecture
it could be called—those caves half-hidden in mist.
I presumed they must be housing
someone, or something, if only the iguanas
when they quit searching for food.
Which was more magnificent, the colors

of the glittering sea or the colors
of the beetling hills, a kind of architecture
which surely somewhere must contain food.
Trees seemed to drift in and out of the mist
as if playing hide and seek with the iguanas.
Maybe the trees could furnish housing—

a lean-to of fallen branches or a tree house.
I kept getting distracted by the colors
of whatever it was the iguanas
were chasing. The architecture
of their bodies so lovely in the mist
I almost forgot I, too, needed food.

What would I find in this barren waste for food—
surely that was more important than housing
for the day was warm, though shrouded by mist
and I was beginning to hallucinate in colors
I'd never seen, unbelievable architecture,
Gaudi-esque buildings that writhed like iguanas.

Couldn't bring myself to eat the iguanas
no matter how desperate I was for food.
I rambled through the mirage of architecture
imagining all the available free housing
and wondering what color
to paint each room: seafoam, eggshell, mist.

Lost in the mist amidst the iguanas
all colors appeared to be food
for thought, housing an utterly new architecture.

January
· — — —

The polar vortex
the shower froze
no honey no eggs no bread
everyone had the flu
explosive bombogenesis
in Florida it rained iguanas

We were never made to last
or was it *We were never meant*
to survive Audre Lorde wrote
Sudden thaw the Mohawk
floods the Stockade again
Man Buried in Wave of Mud

You can't see a shooting star
where you're looking only
in your side vision
Super blue blood moon
Like everyone I squandered
my youth and good intentions

Jeanne et Moi (or, Two Degrees)

`. — — . — — — . — — — . — — —`

I watched *Jules et Jim* again last night.
Jeanne Moreau still captivating
though her character, Catherine,
is monstrous. Jules et Jim
are idiots. The best part is when
Jules, oblivious to Catherine's
changing face, quotes Baudelaire
to Jim——*Woman is natural, therefore
abominable*——and she jumps into the Seine.

One of Moreau's lovers was my grad
school teacher, drop-dead
gorgeous in his rakish youth.
He took me to the Hamptons
for a chaste weekend at Lichtenstein's
estate where I sat next to a Greek prince
in my thrift-shop dress of rotting lace.
Now he is very old and la Moreau
is dead, but for a moment someone
who'd slept with her wanted to marry me.

Man Bun Ken

—.—　　—.—　　—.—

Poor Man Bun Ken, getting teased
on Twitter. Will mean girls make Man Bun Ken
kill himself? (They've been mutilating

Barbie for years.) Who will ever buy
Man Bun Ken, a steal at only nine
ninety-nine. All those Man Bun Kens

interred in the catacombs of Walmart
& Target in plastic-wrapped
sarcophagi, discounted to nothing

or shipped off to Asia where men can wear buns
& not look like twits. It's not easy
being a guy in a Barbie-world.

He was always only an accessory:
who ever actually cared for Ken
in his painted-on trunks & terry-lined

Hawaiian beach jacket? Now Ken comes
in three sizes: Original, Broad & Slim
like a cigarette; seven skin tones, eight

hair colors & nine hairstyles: Corn Row Ken
Buzz Cut Ken, Shaggy Dog Ken & Quiff
(whatever that is) Ken… "Give it up, Ken—

we've been there before," says *Teen Vogue*. "You've got
to find yourself, the *real* you." The real Ken,
alas, ODed on heroin

decades ago. Future archaeologists
may stumble upon his simulacra
& mistake him for a shape-shifting god,

the cyclically dying & reborn
consort of the Great Goddess Barbie.

The Knitting of the Dead

—.—   —.—   —.—   —.—   —.—

There was a flood.

Forgive her, aunties and great-aunties—
she did not know
the cedar chest in the basement got swamped.
She cannot face the stain, the stench.

Where are those unhappy heirlooms now?

The hopeless chest
waits at the foot of her bed
where neglect guilt regret decay
bloom silent as mold in the dark.

Pandora released all evils to fly abroad

but slammed the lid on hope
to save us. Which makes no sense.
Wouldn't the thing with feathers
need to be set free to do its work?

She will open her gift, she swears.

It will fit perfectly.

Lot's Ex

.—.. .—..

Valentine's Day is slippery.
Warming-hut lot empty near dusk.
Snow refrozen to a glazed crust,
cross-country tracks mini twin luges.

Poling my way out of a wood,
over my crunching Splitkeins, I hear
a deep voice behind: Are you
blazing a trail for me? I turn.

Oh, it's *you*, he says, startled.
He's put on weight but still
gains on me. I step back, let him
pass. He mutters, How ya doin'.

I still have his old box of wax.
This year I lost the cork.
I still have his son.
There's the rub, the knot.

He turns left at the six birches
toward the abandoned house
and big hill. Mind racing
No one's here but us

He's faster My bamboo poles
might break. Turning back,
my old wooden skis
catch and I fall.

Sweaty, breathing hard,
only at the car do I look back—
the sky flushed deep rose
and violet behind the trees' black lace.

How the Light Gets In
.—.. .—.. .—.. .—.. .—..

Don't call it your bad hip—
recall the Japanese art of *kintsugi*
and be the cracked vessel
patched with gold.

Don't wince when it squeaks
but thank the bright steel
cupping your pelvis
and capping your thigh.

Don't be shamed by the scar—
you've wrestled till day break
with man and god, and managed
to limp away blessed.

Maria Lactans

— — — — — —

Mothers of America, nurse for as long as you like.
                                        The soul grows by touch.

Ignore your friends' concern
                            that you'll accompany your son to college.
Forget Oedipus,
            a well-fed child won't be afraid to roam.

Nurse in public.
                Wear a top so cunningly constructed
that a woman sitting next to you on a plane
                                    asks, while you're nursing,
if that's your grandson.

Nurse until he calls your breasts *nursies*.
                                    Imagine him in middle school
rounding second base
                asking Skylar if he can touch her nursies.

Don't worry about his teeth.
                        They'll be fine.
Don't worry about your wasband or consort.
                                    They're just jealous.
American men are obsessed with nursies.
                            If only more fed to their heart's delight
there'd be less war, more
                        lineaments of satisfied desire.
Less addiction.
            What's an alcoholic
                        but an aging baby with a bottle?

A nation in pain
                    driving itself around high
                                       trying to self-soothe
to sing itself to sleep.

MOAB

— — — —

The mother of all bombs Milton says
was Satan. Child of the devil you agree.
Who but a fallen Morning Star
could conceive of a nine-meter-long
metal dong delivered by parachute
to drop into Earth's exquisite lap—

It felt like the heavens were falling
The earth like a boat in a storm
My ears were deaf We thought the end
of the world had come
     You can see
the mushroom cloud blooming
to music on the phone in your palm
angels
   children
     sky
      London Bridge
Ashes ashes all fall down

Manna

— — — —

After forty years in the desert
you'd think we'd be grateful
but we hankered after meat

and the lost delicatessen
of Egypt. We kvetched
and kvetched till Moses prayed

Kill me now!
          The Nameless One
in reply, sent more than we could eat—
a flock of quail, flying

right into our mouths.
Chased by a course
of plague to kill off

the kvetchadiks.
From this what do we learn,
my stiff-necked people?

That we are historical pains in the ass.
That though lost and wandering
we are miraculously fed.

That just outside the Promised Land
so close we can taste it
we are all condemned.

By Minnehaha Creek

hearing him pick out
Für Elise
the only piece he knew

I cup my hand
in the cardboard box
cast him upon the water
rinse my grey palm in the creek
scrub the grease off on the grass

sawing away
at my first violin
no one can stand to listen

or pour from its plastic bag
an ashenfall
off an arched bridge he loved to paint
watch the ghost-cloud
depart for the sea

Now We Are 15

—. —. —. —. —.

Driving him to school I say
What's the new word for the year?
In his new low voice he growls
It's still penis.

But it's not. It's sexy.
I'm sexy. The cats are sexy.
Meanwhile he wants to kill his father.
Freud did not make this stuff up.

The only thing he wants for his birthday
is PlayStation 4, so after school
we hit Best Buy. They're all loaded
with Call of Duty: Infinite Warfare.

Boys his age and younger are impressed
as soldiers, girls used as slaves.

I can't believe how old you are! I say.
Did you want me to die when I was 10?

Back home he breaks out Infinite
Warfare, calls the cats strumpets,
says Magical Star's having his baby,
wants to know where I've hidden my penis.

Naming the Animals
—. —. —. —. —. —. —.

In pushing other species to extinction, humanity is busy
sawing off the limb on which it is perched.
—Paul Ehrlich

Angel Island mouse
Bramble Car melomys
Caribbean monk seal
Dusky seaside sparrow
Eastern cougar

Formosan clouded leopard, 2013. *A forest with clouded leopards*
and a forest without clouded leopards mean something different
said Chiang Po-jen, after searching 13 years in vain. *A forest without*
clouded leopards is dead.

Gloomy tube-nosed bat
Hawaiian crow
Ivory-billed woodpecker
Javan tiger

Kaua'i 'o'o. In 1987, the last male was recorded singing his sweet, bell-like
mating call.

Little blue macaw
Madeiran large white butterfly
New Zealand greater short-tailed bat
One-striped opossum

Passenger pigeon. Martha died alone at 1 p.m., Sept. 1, 1914,
in the Cincinnati Zoo.
Pinta Island tortoise. Early June 24, 2012, Lonesome George, over 100.
Pyrenean ibex, 2000. Celia, 13, crushed by a falling tree. Cloned from
Celia's ear, her daughter, born by goat surrogate, lived seven minutes.

Quagga, 1883. The last South African zebra died in an Amsterdam zoo.

Rabb's fringe-limbed tree frog. Sept. 26, 2016. Toughie sired tadpoles
        in captivity, but none survived.

Sea mink
Thylacine, or Tasmanian tiger
Urania sloanus
Vaquita, little cow, the smallest porpoise
Western black rhino
Xerces blue butterfly

Yangtze river dolphin, 2006. Small, white, delicate,
        nearly blind, the goddess of the Yangtze was revered
        as the reincarnation of a drowned princess.

Zanzibar leopard, 1996. Exterminated by Tanzanian villagers
        who believed it the familiar of witches.

Four species an hour.

On a Scale of One to Ten

— — —   — — —   — — —   — — —

This will hurt the doctor says
but it's nothing. Maybe labor
hurts so much to make

everything after seem easy, even
the fourth trimester

which could drive anyone to suicide
infanticide, right off
the charts. There is one pain

you don't dare contemplate
(though it used to be
commonplace):

loss of a child. Yours
wants to be a scientist. You sit
together on the couch watching *Nova*:

Lush vegetation rings an ancient lake
where mammoths graze, animated

wooly elephants with Dr. Seuss tusks
long and curling. The whole herd
fossilized under a dry lakebed.

What caused their sudden death?

Scientists pour water onto a tray
of sand, let it sink, place a carved

elephant on the dry crust. They pick up
the table's four corners and shake
to make earthquake:

water bubbles up,
the toy sinks
to its knees. Quicksand. Cut

to an animated mammoth
baby trapped at her side

trunks waving
helplessly.
                Who can stand this

100,000-year-old pain
the kabillions of animals

from then to now, each single
suffering being
snuffed out—

            Next on *Nova*:
nebulae give birth to galaxies of stars.

Ode to Ibolya
— — — — — —

I.

Her grave's an empty stage, velvet curtains drawn.
Ravens trace the map of Transylvania:
their cries like grinding wheels
sharpen the clouds
scrawl arabesques on the sky.
Its taste of snow and arsenic
its scent of forget-me-nots.
The dark granite looms
like a rhapsody in a box. Locked.

The filthy pocketknife of convention
cut her off. The chatty village
spat her out, a cherry stone.
Ibolya sails hard above the hillside
beyond the cemetery
upside-down and single
among the chickens cows candlesticks
and her secret aristocratic lover.

Basia looks like her, Aunt Klari says
and will also be unlucky in love.
But not that bad. Her foxy diamonds
slip off her fingerbones. True love
is a graveyard, as all ballads know.

II.

Ibolya means Violet. She bloomed
1896 to 1919, in Margita
Hungary (Romania now).
Her sister Erzsi found her
wilted with arsenic on their mother's grave
and fled to Cleveland. The third sister
Anya, followed, as in a fairy tale—
the rest, who stayed, ended
in ovens. Aunt Klari says
Only by Ibolya, by her unhappy love
are we alive, *kein ayin hara.*

Vaksn zolstu vi a tsibele mitn kop in dr'erd:
May you grow like an onion, with your head
in the ground. Her cracked photograph
still curses that faithless man (who was
perhaps just a married pharmacist?).
Her shadowed eyes recite their litany
as her elegant dress rereads
Madame Bovary on that lonely hill,
her solitary window shut tight.

Like a rhapsody in a box, locked
the dark granite looms.
Its scent of forget-me-nots
its taste of snow and arsenic
scrawl arabesques on the sky
sharpen the clouds.
Their cries like grinding wheels
ravens trace the map of Transylvania.
Her grave's an empty stage, velvet curtains drawn.

Painlandia
.— —. .— —.

You want only to escape
barefoot, schlepping

your bundle. If you're lucky
and do, you lose the lingo

we all want only to forget.
Cross the border and no one

gets that primitive tongue
that sounds to them like barking

or moaning. Who could guess
the tenderness of its ten thousand

untranslatable ways of saying
Feel.

Poem

.— —.

Our old friend Emilio from Milan said,
When the end comes I'll climb a mountain
to watch with a good red wine,
wearing my father's yellow kid gloves.

We'd met him on a boat to Bora Bora.
La dolce vita—ah, we were so young
and so in love. And then, we weren't.

Emilio, this poem is for you—
my yellow gloves, red wine, mountain.

Can I call the man free whom a woman governs?
　　　　　—Cicero

Positively West Fourth Street
.— —. . — —. .— —. .— —. . — —.

She wanders the West Village, no longer
remembering which street leads to which, stares
up at buildings, trying to pick out old
apartments—was that the balcony where

she smashed his beeper? Is that the bloody
apartment on Carmine Street where love
at first sight ended in a black eye?
Everyone else stares down at their phones

or huddles in pairs over maps. Whole tour
groups on foot, like ducklings, or in double-
decker busses, pointing out where Dylan
leaned against Suze Rotolo on Jones

Street... John's Pizza's still there,
Matt Umanov Guitars—the rest
new restaurants she never cried in, posh shops
full of smug young things with tiny dogs—she's lost

as any tourist, here in her own past
full of compassion for the young stranger
who knew so little and was about to
learn so much.

There would be nothing missing from my happiness had I always been missing a wife ...
All husbands know this.
  —Foreoneus, King of the Greeks, qtd in Walter Map

Quoth the Queane
— —.— — —.— — —.—

We'll quash your quietude.

We'll quibble till you quiver.

We'll question your quality.

We'll quarrel till you quake.

We'll quicken without a qualm.

We'll quell your quest.

We'll quench your quirks.

We'll quiet your quandary.

We'll queer your quickie.

We'll quarry you a new quarry.

We'll quilt your quietus.

Quintessence of the quotidian?

We quit.

She Drives Home
after Viewing the Drones Quilt

— —.— — —.— — —.— — —.— — —.—

Izaak, age 12

on the couch playing games on his phone.
His sneakers the neon colors of tropical fish.
His flesh knitting sweetly on long, milk-fed bones.
His $3,000 braces.
She hugs him till she feels the bird beating in its cage
    of ribs

while all those little ones—
    Noor Aziz, age 8
    Shafiq, age 2
    Shakira, age 4
    Sheika, age 3
    Ikramullah Zada, age 12
    Khadije Ali, age 1—
have flown forever out of reach

to keep her tank full.
Her house warm. Her neighbors
blowing dead leaves off the lawn.

All night the hollow moan of oil trains
runs hidden behind trees in the dark.

Rondeau for Shaimaa al-Sabbagh

·—· ·—· ·—· ·—· ·—· ·—· ·—· ·—· ·—·

We have a little sister ...
And if she be a door,
We will enclose her with boards of cedar.
——Song of Songs 8:8-9

Their birdshot pierced the lung and heart
of a songbird. Its simple start
the spring chant—*freedom justice bread*—
and a wreath of flowers for the dead
of Tahrir Square. Playing their part

masked police fired on her party
with guns and gas. Her eyes smarted
yet she stood till her face streamed red.
Their birdshot pierced

her. A friend caught her fall, departed
bearing all her unmade years and art.
Bullets fired close-range in crowded
Cairo—narrow streets choked with dread
where this young woman poet bled
to death. Long-range, too, our hearts
their birdshot pierced.

Researchers Turn Spinach into Heart

.—. .—. .—. .—. .—. .—. .—. .—. .—. .—.

Popeye wouldn't blink—
spinach ever his canned salvation.
In my hometown, Worcester
they're washing spinach

in detergent, seeding
the white translucent leaves
with cardiac tissue. After day five
the leaf begins to beat.

They're also using parsley, sweet wormwood
and hairy peanut root. The hollow stem
of jewelweed could be for arteries
and wood or bamboo for bone.

Spinach is not the only superfood.
In Ottawa they're growing scary
human ears out of apple slices.
Like Popeye always says, *I yam what I yam.*

Sheer
... ...

I have lost friends, some by death ...
others by sheer inability to cross the street.
                        —Virginia Woolf

I'd just left your old studio on West 4th Street for the last time.
Where you moved when we fell in love. We lived on $5 Cuban-Chinese
chicken and even cheaper wine, haunted the used bookstores that used
to grace Manhattan. It was so sunny when I went up to say goodbye—
you and your beautiful young blonde wife packing up, moving to her
house in Carroll Gardens—I put my sunglasses on and ran down the dark
red staircase past the Pink Pussycat, its window full of black leather and
chains I never looked back at. It was even darker outside, just starting to
pour. Fumbling with a collapsible umbrella, I began to dash across West
4th when a bike delivery guy shouted so loud,

NO!

I froze
            as if playing statue—
                                    the ball of one foot half off the curb
the other mid-stride as wind slapped my face, the trail of a black SUV
the size of Oklahoma stampeding past.

Thank you! I cried. Not being dead yet. My guardian angel gone,
to bring someone pizza. I fixed the umbrella, looked both ways, and
walked on water across the street.

Souvenir

... ...

On an almost hidden
shelf of
a curiosity shop
in a crystal cup
sloped
like a martini glass
a small fish
thrashed—
maybe a baby
ornamental
carp—

and a white dove also
submerged
tiny as a hummingbird
beat its
panicking
wings

Affixed to the cup
a card said
This is
Real

The wings of the dove
underwater
beating—
the terrified eyes—
this souvenir
I bring back
for you

Save Our Ship
... ...

Your clamshell rings and rings
                              wrapped in seagreen plastic

        Mer-crone calling Fisher King

The number you are calling has a voice mailbox that has been deluged

        A drowned sailor picks up

... crusts of dried salt in the streets ...
                              you're breaking up ...
        The tide of pink jellyfish
                              big as washing machines
                                                rises

Ocean's hurricane voice calling back
                                    could crush your skull
        Wake up!   Wake up!   Wake up!

You've overslept all your calendars are drowned

        The only road is disappearing beneath the sea

the inundation   has begun
                of the coast
                        the sea is now so near the brim

SOS

         ... ‾ ‾ ... ... ‾ ‾ ... ... ‾ ‾ ... ... ‾ ‾ ... ... ‾ ‾ ... ... ‾ ‾ ...
... ‾ ‾ ... ... ‾ ‾ ... ... ‾ ‾ ... ... ‾ ‾ ... ... ‾ ‾ ... ... ‾ ‾ ... ... ‾ ‾ ...
... ‾ ‾ ... ... ‾ ‾ ... ... ‾ ‾ ... ... ‾ ‾ ... ... ‾ ‾ ... ... ‾ ‾ ... ... ‾ ‾ ...
... ‾ ‾ ... ... ‾ ‾ ... ... ‾ ‾ ... ... ‾ ‾ ... ... ‾ ‾ ... ... ‾ ‾ ... ... ‾ ‾ ...
... ‾ ‾ ... ... ‾ ‾ ... ... ‾ ‾ ... ... ‾ ‾ ... ... ‾ ‾ ... ... ‾ ‾ ... ... ‾ ‾ ...
... ‾ ‾ ... ... ‾ ‾ ... ... ‾ ‾ ... ... ‾ ‾ ...... ‾ ‾ ... ... ‾ ‾ ... ... ‾ ‾ ...
... ‾ ‾ ... ... ‾ ‾ ... ... ‾ ‾ ... ... ‾ ‾ ...... ‾ ‾ ... ... ‾ ‾ ... ... ‾ ‾ ...

Shooting into the Hurricane

... ‒ ‒ ‒ ...   ... ‒ ‒ ‒ ...   ... ‒ ‒ ‒ ...

Some guy posted
Shoot at Hurricane Irma
stunned when tens
of thousands signed up.

A sheriff tweeted DO NOT
shoot @ Irma. You won't make it
turn around & very dangerous
side effects. We laughed

gave you the Darwin Award
said you put the duh in Florida
for shooting at the hurricane
when the bullet boomeranged

back into your brain.
We felt better about our laughter
when we heard you were fake.

We laughed but keep following
fake-news you, our bellwether,
off the Wile E. Coyote cliff—

Spiritual Housekeeping

··· ··· ··· ··· ··· ··· ··· ···

Dust meditation daily.

Keep desires from cluttering counter
    or worries piling up in sink.

Water the light.

Shake beliefs regularly
    and beat with a broom in snow.

Commune with spirits lingering in closets.

Make a bottle tree to chase demons away
    from aprons and spoons.

Spare all spiders.

Scrub the soul on hands and knees
    as needed.

Defrost fears.

Don't forget to vacuum under the id.

Life can only be understood backwards, but it must be lived forwards.
—Kierkegaard

This Life

— — — —

is a novel you find hard to put down.
Often you stay up too late at night
reading. You never flip
to the back to see how it ends.
Willing suspension of disbelief.

All this foreshadowing
and dramatic irony—lost
on you till it's too late.

You try to slow down, yet once
you're halfway through, the pages
turn themselves, whole chapters race.

Like Emma, you're blind
to your own designs,
can't sort the plot from your
blunders. Some found elements
and erasure, a bit experimental.

No thriller. No *War and Peace*
or *Brothers K*, but who'd
want to live in those?

In bed, weary, you let it drop
each night. When you open your eyes
there it is again.

To You, U
..— ..— ..—

You dictated my place in line, near the end,
in class, at the back, far as Timbuktu
or Ultima Thule, close as my middle name,
Louise. You begin the universe, true-blue
symbol of union in Venn diagrams & geometry.

In the U.K. you appear in colour
labour, honour, but not in the U.S.
though you stand for united, uranium
& university. You can be Absolut
in vodka & virtue, luxe as in furs & cruelty.

Untrackable as Dersu Uzala
you moved here from Phoenicia
via Upsilon and V. Doubled
you make W, as in makin' whoopee
or those Unitarians called U-U's.

U R I & I M U, ultimate umbilicus,
root of everything, the ur— and its
negation: undone, unmanned, unmade.
Uncountable, beyond number, umpteenth.
Ulterior to utterance, you ululate.

Uncanny U-haul of memory
with everything crammed inside.
Unending as a hula hoop,
Uroboros, you swallow
yourself up utterly.

Venus with a Mirror
...— ...— ...— ...— ...—

After Titian

Love expects her own radiance to last
forever.
       Her large soft body
doughy belly and arms
no woman today would want
                    but the face—
supermodel gorgeous
              framed
by golden curls braided with pearls—
looks over her shoulder.
              Behind her
a cherub's about to bonk her over the head
with a wreath.
            Beside her
another sturdy cherub holds up
the heavy mirror.

              Between them
                   the vertical
slice of her
          trapped in the mirror
                    doesn't match—
one large dark eye
             spooked
like a horse
          the flesh beneath sags
                   She sees
what any woman sees
            in a mirror
her worst
        The old woman
                  rising toward her
a goblin shark
          The dark wood frame
                  closing
a coffin lid.

For Vincent Byrne
...— ...— ...— ...—

How old were we
when we read together
at Cornelia St. Café?
You seemed old to me then (surely
no older than I am now) so I
must have been young.

Are you still there? I tried
to find you online, failed,
bought your three books.
You'd come from Dublin,
studied for priesthood,
three kids, divorced, Rye
New York—advertising
kept *the wolf out of doors.*

If I found you, what
would I say—that upon one
hearing, three of your poems
became part of me? One
about always looking for milk
in the hardware store.
Another, falling in love
with yourself at an art show.

In the third, about to gas yourself
but ashamed of the grimy oven
you scrub it clean
sip a glass of claret
by candlelight and Vivaldi
glowing with virtue.

If this world survives
another quarter century
will anyone come looking
for me, and who will remember
three of my poems?

Golden Orb Weaver

.— — .— — .— — .— —

Banana Spider waits in the garden
yellow legs elegant
in black thigh-highs.

She signs her day's work like Zorro
a zigzag of bold white Z's
for Zipper Spider. Or

sideways, W's, for wisdom
women's arts and war
Athena's mark.

Like Penelope, she rips
out her work each night
to redo every day. Her gossamer's

shapely and dangerous
someone's shroud:
you could lose yourself

wake wrapped in silk
good as dead.
The beauty of her web

mandala of the almost
unseen, draws you in.
How it glints in the light

then disappears. Hinting
at what is always there
unnoticed. The Writing Spider.

Poised on her neat work
she sits in the center
and lets loose.

Wyndemoan

.— — .— — .— —

We go down in darkness
  we go tilt-

    a-whirling away from our star
      into cold space

Persephone descends
  the marble stair

    cold feet cold hands
      cold bed

Leaves whisper Japanese
  death poems

    like the snow our end too
      is coming my love

X-Wife
—··— —··—

Whose car is parked in your drive—
how everyone knows who you're seeing.
How your ex must seethe when he
drops off the kid. Late for work again
you're stuck behind his despised SUV
all the way to the freeway, trapped
on the back routes he taught you.
An iron band constricts heart to gut—
Möbius strip of love-turned-hate.

You can't evade him or this commute,
these years on the chain gang
of shared custody. Fall back,
keep him in front—he could ram
you from behind. Cars intervene, peel
aside, till your windshield faces
his bumper again, each of you steeled.

So clear in the rearview the impending
wreck of your marriage—the slow-mo
inevitable slide to crash, wrangling
over damages, whiplash that lingers
for years. From your 16-year-old
Honda, your ex-wife X-ray vision can see
all the way inside to the wounded
3-year-old manoeuvering his tank.

Your Mother Serves Tongue
—.— —   —.— —   —.— —   —.— —

How could you
put another creature's tongue
into your mouth? How could you
bite, chew, swallow?

Cannibal. Obscene.
How could you
tell the difference

between a cow's tongue and its delicious
rump? How could you tell
the difference between
a cow's tongue and your own?

Our tongues could speak.
The poor cow's couldn't—
how it ended up on the supper table.

But could a young girl speak?
Smile, men said. *Cat got
your tongue?* Who
had swallowed yours? No one

had attacked you yet
or even exposed himself
yet you already knew

the tale of Philomel
endlessly repeating like DNA
enfolded within that mute slab,
the unspeakable on a platter

on the table of white Formica
speckled with gold. Your mother
urging you, *Try just one bite.*

After Zumba
— —.. — —..

We see women tossing pink and white
sprays of gladioli, snapdragons and lilies
into dumpsters behind the Dance Museum.
Guess the guests didn't want them.
We dive in: dead-head, snip the stems,
fill the whole house with bloom.

So what if some snaps droop
and their pink mouths aren't so perky.
We, too, have gone soft and a bit brown
around the edges. We've had our wedding
feasts—clutched the fated bouquets
and tossed them—some more than once.

So what if the bloom is off—the rose
is still a rose. Someone said the Dalai Lama's
flowers last longer than anyone's.
He changes the water and trims
the stems every day. He speaks to them
and each blossom listens.

Notes

"The Diverse Vices of Women, Alphabetized" was written by Archbishop Antoninus of Florence in 1454 to teach women to control their sensual appetites, especially their desire for speech. It expands upon Giovanni Dominici's earlier alphabet, which is in turn based upon Ecclesiasticus, a book included in the Catholic and Orthodox bibles. Many of the epigraphs throughout this book come from these sources. Antoninus was canonized in 1523.

"Endnotes to Coral Reefs" is mostly a found poem, from *Coral Reefs*, Lesley A. DuTemple, and "Climate-Related Death of Coral Around World Alarms Scientists," *New York Times*, 4/10/2016.

"How the Light Gets In": The title is from Leonard Cohen's song "Anthem." *Kintsugi* is the Japanese art of mending pottery with gold.

"How It Happens" responds to "Explain the Rob Porter Story. Any of It," Ruth Marcus, *Washington Post*, 2/7/2018.

"I Go on the Road of All the Earth" is mostly a found poem, from "Evidence of Evil," Timothy W. Ryback, *The New Yorker*, 11/15/1993.

"MOAB" is an acronym for Massive Ordnance Air Blast bomb (the GBU-43/B), nicknamed the Mother of All Bombs, dropped on Afghanistan by the U.S. under President Trump, Thurs., April 13, 2017. In *Paradise Lost*, Satan invents ordnance.

"Naming the Animals" is mostly a found poem, from the Center for Biological Diversity's website and various other lists of extinct animals. At the time of writing, the vaquita was critically endangered, with two dozen believed yet to survive.

"Positively West Fourth Street": Matt Umanov Guitars has since been replaced by The Loyal restaurant, *The New Yorker*, 1/8/2018.

"She Drives Home after Viewing the Drones Quilt": Inspired by the AIDS Quilt, and begun by women working for peace in the U.K., the Drones Quilt commemorates civilians killed by U.S. drones.

"Rondeau for Shaimaa al-Sabbagh": "A left-leaning poet and activist, 32, was killed in Cairo … birdshot fired at close range had pierced her lung and heart," "At Least 18 Killed in Violence," *New York Times*, 1/26/2015.

"Researchers Turn Spinach into Heart" is mostly a found poem, from "Researchers Turn Spinach Leaves Into Beating Heart Tissues," Jason Daley, *Smithsonian*, 3/27/2017.

*

"The Other Barbara" is for Barbara Abrams and Barbara Ehrlich Glaser.

"The Knitting of the Dead" is in memory of Aunt Renée Katz and Great-Aunt Frieda Katz.

"*Maria Lactans*" is for Frank Bidart and Frank O'Hara.

"Manna" is for rabbis Linda Motzkin and Jonathan Rubenstein.

"By Minnehaha Creek" is in memory of my father, Frank Ungar.

"Ode to Ibolya" is in memory of aunts Klari, Vera, and Bea Ungar, who told us tales of the Old Country.

"Poem" is for Emilio and Monica Calcagni.

"After Zumba" is for Laurie Zabele Cawley and the Zumba crew.